Open Arms:
The Steve Perry Anthology

I'd like to specially thank...Lora Beard, Cyndy Poon, Tim McQuaid, John Stix, Lee Phillips, Gabrielle Fastman, and John Jackson, for without their help and support—this book would not have happened.
Thank you all...Steve Perry

Cover photo by Paul Natkin

Cherry Lane Music Company
Director of Publications/Project Editor: Mark Phillips
Manager of Publications: Gabrielle Fastman

ISBN-13: 978-1-57560-711-5
ISBN-10: 1-57560-711-5

Visit our website at www.cherrylane.com 

CONTENTS

Steve Perry: The Interview

by John Stix

Give me a picture of "Any Way You Want It."

It's from the *Departure* album. It was recorded in a studio in San Francisco. It was inspired by watching Phil Lynott of Thin Lizzy, who opened for us on tour. I loved his ability and phrasing. This guy is one of the more under-recognized geniuses of that era. He inspired the original seed of the song, which has a guitar/vocal interchange: "She loves to laugh," guitar riff, "she loves to sing," guitar riff, "she does everything," guitar riff. It grew from there. Phil was a real poet; he was a frightening genius.

Did you plan the song with an a cappella vocal part?

No. That was a last-minute thing. There is a vocal cluster in the chorus. I'm not sure of the exact inversions, but I found them in my head and sang them against each other. I was grateful to have Gregg Rolie there, who supported them and would come up with additional vocal clusters, too. Those vocal clusters—the notes that were chosen—are really unique and give the chorus its sort of timeless quality.

"Don't Fight It" is your most visible duet.

I really wanted to write with Kenny Loggins. He had written some great music with Michael McDonald just previous to this, and his own material was always stunning. The time presented itself during a short break during a Journey tour. We sat down to write in his music room off to the side of the house. We were going to write something for his upcoming record. I had a bass guitar; he had a guitar. Nothing really happened. I think he was trying to do what an artist often does when he knows what his album needs, which is to write in a certain needed direction. We are all guilty of that sometimes. I felt like I was being pulled somewhere creatively—but I didn't know what it was he was looking for.

Is it difficult because you have to be creative on the spot?

Yes. I have never been an on-demand guy. When it's raining it really influences me. And when the sun is shining it influences me. I'm not able

PHOTO: WILLIAM HAMES

to write sunshine songs during the rain or rain songs during the sunshine. I am sort of stuck with wherever pulls me at the time. And there I was with him, being pulled in an area where I thought maybe I'm not so comfortable. I could see he was getting frustrated, and I think he would admit to this being true. He got up and said, "I'll be right back," and he went into the main house. I sat there and thought that maybe this wasn't going as well as it could, and I started thumping on the bass this pattern: [sings] "Don't fight it, don't fight it. It will only do you good." He came walking in and I was doing that. He sat down and grabbed the guitar and started playing along with me. He said, "What is that?" I said, "While you were gone, it was something I was thumping on." I could see that he liked it.

Did you record the vocals face to face?

No, I went back on tour and he went in with his producer Bruce Botnick and recorded the track. I loved the track when I heard it. He put Neil Geraldo, originally with Pat Benatar, on guitar. I still think he is one of the most naturally talented geniuses around. When I got a break in the tour, I flew out to do my vocals. Kenny was in the control room with Bruce as I sang my parts against what he had already laid down. That was the first duet I had done. I recently did another one.

You're talking about "A Brand New Start," which is also in this book.

"A Brand New Start" was written by me and David Pack, previously the lead singer/songwriter from Ambrosia. I always admired their songs and I definitely admired David's voice. I thought maybe someday we could get together, and all of a sudden the opportunity presented itself. I got a hold of him and then 9/11 happened and the anthrax scare was showing up everywhere across the United States. The country was in a lot of fear. It brought out in me a certain truth about how some of my relationships have fallen apart because of my lack of willingness to make some big changes. If you really listen to the lyrics, you will see that is the honest admission. "You tried to reach something you could not touch. Maybe there in the end we'll find we both cared too much. Here's where our blue skies sadly turn dark. We were almost a part of a brand new start." The idea that "you tried to reach something you could not touch" means I'm accessible but only to a certain point. That was probably one of the deepest admissions to date of some of my personal emotional limits.

"Don't Stop Believin'" sounds like two different songs put together.

It is an unorthodox arrangement because it does have several choruses. The "strangers waiting" section is arguably a chorus unto itself. Then it has a second "Don't Stop Believin'" outro chorus. It is one of the more different songs that Jon Cain, Neal Schon, and I ever wrote. Between Neal and I, we came up with the guitar/bass line. Jon Cain had the keyboard part started, and out of that came the melody. Later Jon and I sat down and wrote the lyrics from our own experiences. He being a Chicago boy and me remembering what it was like being in Detroit on tour the year before and seeing people down on the street at three or four in the morning, below my hotel room, still out creeping around looking for some more emotion somewhere. I never forgot that. That is where it came from with "Just a small town girl livin' in a lonely world. She took the midnight train going anywhere." I always loved trains. There was no commercial airport in my little hometown, but there was a train and the train represented freedom.

Were you surprised the song has had a strong second life?

I am stunned that it has done so well. I have to give credit to not only Journey but also to many people like program directors across the country who continue to play it while the landscape of music evolves and changes around it. At the same time there were people like film director Patty Jenkins [*Monster*]. Though she is an admitted punker from the original hardcore scene, she said she was also a closet Steve Perry/Journey fan. She loved this song from the first day she heard it. But she never could tell anybody because she was a hardcore punker. Patty loved skating to this song when she was a punker living in Lawrence, Kansas. When she wrote and directed *Monster*, starring Charlize Theron, she decided to use this song in the background during the first kissing scene in the roller rink. That scene became one of the launching points of the film. A year or two later, another generation found the song by seeing it on *Laguna Beach*. A whole new generation has since embraced this song and that's a very cool thing.

What more could you want than to see it transition across all these generations and musical genres as time changes?

This is the biggest gift a singer/songwriter could ever want. It was one of those songs that definitely came together in a George Martin fashion, in the studio. It was built. It was arranged to be sectional and have a chorus that was to be dwarfed only by the outro chorus. All those decisions were made in the writing and arranging process. But in the studio is where those sections had to truly stand on their own and be definitive unto themselves. The requirement, recording-wise and performance-wise, was demanding. But once it was achieved, Neal Schon came up with brilliant guitar parts.

I never knew it until later, but it sounds like a train on the tracks: *diga diga diga*. Then the second verse kicks in: "A singer in a smokey room. The smell of wine and cheap perfume." I was that singer in a smokey room. I used to play nightclubs and it was exactly like that. The smell of wine and cheap perfume was everywhere. You bet your ass "for a smile you could share the night." And did that not, and does it not still, go on.... and on.... and on? It will forever go on. There are certain things that I've lived through that Jon Cain lived through and people continue to live through, because it's all just part of the rites of passage in this world.

"Faithfully" is another important song for Journey.

It was the closing song for all Journey shows and for my solo tour. That song was written solely by Jonathan Cain. I remember we were in the rehearsal hall in the East Bay of San Francisco, and he walked in with his demo. In the studio is where this one came alive. There was a certain thing I had emotionally when I sang the verses that I didn't have on any ballad I had done before. I think it was written in his key, which gave me a tone that brought out a certain emotion in me. When I sang the word *faithfully* at the very end, I reached for a note that was truly a cry out to my girlfriend at the time. If she could only hear it, if she could only believe that this is exactly how I felt, maybe her fears would go away.

What about the *whoa's* near the end, where you and Neal echo each other?

They were all studio moments; nothing was written. It's about the environment of the studio; you are able to watch certain tracks become bigger than life, right in front of your eyes. A song goes from rehearsal to a track, and when it moves to a well-performed track, it's magic.

Was Neal doing that with you in the studio?

He had done that outro thing. He played and I answered to him. I stopped when he was playing and then sang when he wasn't. I don't know how much of that was choreographed in rehearsal. But it instinctively happened in the studio. Let me tell you something you don't know. After this song was a hit, we got a tape from the management of Prince. There was a song called "Purple Rain," and the manager said this was going to be the title of his upcoming film. They were concerned about releasing it, thinking we might come after them for copyright infringement. We were given this cassette in advance of the release of the film, to make sure there were not going to be any problems. Prince had inadvertently used the same chord changes as in the outro of "Faithfully." Though he was singing the words "purple rain" over them, they were still the same changes. I remember Neal and Jon saying, "It's okay." I thought that if they're okay with it, then so was I so we told them it would not be a problem.

Tell me the story behind "Patiently."

I was living in L.A. at the time. Craig Krampf, a drummer friend of mine, put together a group with Steve Delacey on guitar, and Richard Michaels Haddad on bass and myself. We called ourselves the Alien Project. We were also called Street Talk for a while because there was talk on the street about this band. Unfortunately, the bass player, Richard, was in a fatal car accident during the 4th of July weekend. The next week we were supposed to talk about contracts with two major labels. I was shattered, as were the rest of the guys. He was so good that he was irreplaceable. A few weeks went by, and then I got a call from Don Ellis, who was running Columbia Records on the West Coast. He said, "I'm sorry to hear about your bass player" and he let me know how much he loved the band. Then he said, "We want to know if you would be at all interested in checking out this group called Journey, who we made three albums with. They want to make a musical change more towards songwriting. They need a singer and they have been looking, and we think you would be somebody they should check out. We are going to suggest that, if you would be interested." The next thing I knew, I found myself sharing a room with Neal Schon in Denver—where Journey was opening for an ELP tour [Emerson, Lake & Palmer]. That night Neal and I sat in a hotel room and wrote "Patiently." It happened in about ten minutes. The lyrics reflect exactly what was going on with me at that moment, waiting "for your lights to shine on me, for your song inside of me." I really wanted to join the band.

How soon after writing "Patiently" were you offered the gig?

Not right away. They wanted to check me out first. I think the first thing that happened was that I met the band in San Bernardino, where they were opening for Thin Lizzy. I met them backstage and sang them a song I had written, "Lovin', Touchin', Squeezin'." I sang it live in a backstage locker room that had great echo. That was the first time I sang for the band with the hope of being accepted. I love the *na na* part. The *na na's* came later. The song was written and finished. One time on the road, the *na na's* suddenly came out when I was playing the bass with Neal backstage somewhere in America. I just started singing

PHOTO: JOHN SCARPATI

the *na na's*. Gregg Rolie played some of the best rock-and-roll honky-tonk piano on this track. It's reminiscent of Nicky Hopkins. Gregg Rolie instinctively drifted that way on his keyboard parts, and it took the song into a real honky-tonk, bar room, rock-and-roll kind of atmosphere. Brilliant, I'd say!

"Lights" is a San Francisco theme song.

It was originally started in L.A. when I was starving; I couldn't get a gig. Originally, it went "When the lights go down in the city and the sun shines on L.A." That was all I had. I thought it would be a little piece I would sing and they could use it to start the six o'clock news. I just wanted to play music and eat. Shortly thereafter I got the phone call to meet Journey. After I joined the band and we were writing songs for what was to become the *Infinity* album, I pulled that song out and we finished it. I have always loved San Francisco from the very first time I went there, so I switched the lyric to "city by the bay" because that's San Francisco's nickname.

Where is the spark in that one?

I would guess in live performance. I think that's where this song sounded the best. The album version, though it's great, was recorded and assembled with me stacking all my voices and all the parts in a small San Francisco studio called His Masters Wheels, but live it would really open up. The Neal Schon guitar solo is the most definitive "city by the bay" guitar solo I have ever heard come out of San Francisco from that era. I can see the City when I hear his solo.

What's the story behind "Oh Sherrie"?

"Oh Sherrie" was first written by Bill Cuomo on keyboards, Craig Krampf thumping on a drum pad, and myself. We had the whole song—the melody and the idea. I believe I originally thought of having it start a capella, with a single voice. I wanted the opening to be as strong as in the song where I first heard that done, "Bernadette," by the Four Tops. "Bernadette," by itself said so much. I was a kid when I first heard Levi Stubbs scream it out by himself, and I never forgot it. When it came time to write "Oh Sherrie," I wanted the opening line, "Should have been gone," to have that same desperate reaching out. The lyrics weren't done but the music and melodies were all completely finished. Then I sat down with Randy Goodrum and he helped me make sense of some of my phonetic intentions. He was very talented in that way. Some of them almost sounded exactly like what I was trying to say, but I hadn't said it. Together we straightened out the phonetics emotionally into a real personal story. The piano parts in "Oh Sherrie," especially the intro piece that happens before the voice, came from a very prolific keyboardist named Bill Cuomo. He showed up with the idea and his Chroma—an instrument sort of like an electric harpsichord. I loved the sound of it. It had to be the foundational instrument of the song, because it was so beautiful when you plugged it directly into the console or through a Marshall [amp]. Bill wanted to end the song with the Chroma part. I said not only should we end it, we should have the option of starting it that way too, with the a cappella line coming in after it. Bill is truly a genius classical keyboardist.

What do you think about the Journey track "Stone in Love"?

"Stone in Love" is one of my favorite Neal Schon moments. That's an amazing guitar song. The recently released *Live in Houston 1981* DVD really shows the power of those opening guitar parts. I come in and sing the true story of times I remember living in the central San Joaquin Valley. "Those crazy nights I do remember in my youth. I do recall those were the best times most of all." I remember being in Three Rivers, California, by the river where this girl would show up with the shortest washed out, light-blue tattered short shorts. If you were lying on the rocks at Three Rivers she would be standing there and you would just glance to the left and, oh my god, it was the most glorious thing you ever saw in your life. "In the heat with a blue jean girl; burnin' love comes once in a lifetime." I'm telling you, man, it's still magic to me when I think of it. I can see it like it was yesterday. It was so nasty and beautiful. It's what rock 'n' roll is all about to me.

What's the history of "Wheel in the Sky"?

I was with Neal in a pizza parlor on a tour night off. Nobody knew who we were yet. Neal and I were having a pizza. I walk over to the jukebox in the corner and I see "Wheel in the Sky" by Journey on the jukebox. I pulled some quarters out of my pocket and I played the song. I sat down and didn't say anything. I was waiting and waiting and looking at him. The song starts and he doesn't get it at first. All of a sudden he looks at me and turns around and says, "I love this song." And we laughed. That was the first time we had a sense that we had a chance to be big, because we were finally on a jukebox.

Talk about "Who's Crying Now."

I was in L.A. visiting some friends, and was driving up to San Francisco to write with Jonathan Cain. I had my small cassette player in the car as I was driving up Route 99 from L.A. I was listening to the radio and I got tired of what I was hearing and turned it off. In my head, out of nowhere, came the "one love feeds the fire" melody, which ended with "I wonder who's crying now." All I had was the chorus melody with "who's crying now" at the ending of every stanza. I put it on the cassette player, got up to San Francisco, and told Jon, "I've got this idea I was working on, just a sketch of a chorus that came to me on the way up here." Jonathan figured out the chords. That was the first song we wrote together.

It sounds like a duet with Jonathan.

It was sort of the extension of "Lovin', Touchin', Squeezin'": I trusted you, you hurt me, we broke up. I wonder if you're getting what you did to me? This song was the next evolution in songwriting between Jonathan Cain and myself, and it came with a very cool B section: "Only so many tears you can cry till the heartache is over, and now you can say your love will never die." I don't think I heard anybody do that kind of a cappella keyboard voice B section before. It wasn't Jon, it wasn't me, it was us. That was the beginning of our writing careers together.

O: WILLIAM HAMES

It sounds like it happened in the studio.

Steve Smith was just awesome. He was on it immediately. He knew what it needed to be.

"You Better Wait."

That evolved so many times. The lyrics are about a girl who comes to Hollywood and has big dreams. She gets stuck in the dark side of her dreams on the streets of Los Angeles. She goes from Hollywood to the dark side of Hollywood and into downtown L.A. "Stop yourself before you fall." It really is saying you better wait. Because you can see people flipping across their dreams into problems and losing sight of what they came here for.

"Good Morning Girl."

To this day I don't know how this song was sung so easily and how it turned out so emotional. I am stunned when I hear this short little piece. It was originally designed to be a little piece of music to intro "Stay Awhile," but Neal had these guitar chords that I loved so much and I was going through a huge emotional sadness about this girl I truly loved. I think I had a total fantasy of what it would be like if we just woke up in the morning and it was all love and rainbows. It really is about the love I had for her, and I was trying to sing it with the hope that she would feel it. I don't think she really heard it. If she had, it might have saved our relationship.

"Foolish Heart" is also from your solo album *Street Talk*.

This is the first song I ever wrote with Randy Goodrum. I was told by Andy Newmark, a brilliant drummer, "If you ever do a solo album, you've got to get together with this writer named Randy Goodrum." We got together one afternoon. We'd have a cup of coffee and go right into writing and absolutely finishing that song that day, including the lyrics. I had done it a few times, but I got more in the habit of digesting things and rearranging things and going back and working on the lyrics. Randy was a Nashville writer who was used to, as he calls it, "skulling out the lyric." He said, "Let's skull out the lyric right now." I thought: Man, that is pretty rock 'n' roll, 'skull out the lyric.' So we did. We sat and wrote the music in about two hours and wrote the rest of the song in about two hours and went to lunch. It was done. The version on the album is exactly what the demo was from our four hour writing session.

"Melody" is a sweet song.

Years had gone by and Randy Goodrum had moved to Los Angeles. I went over to his new house one evening and "Melody" was born. He played the melody on the piano and I answered it. It was one of those musical duets between voice and piano, and to this day people who've heard it on my *Steve Perry Greatest Hits* CD stop me and tell me that it's one of their favorite songs. I always thought that should have been a single. I later had my falling out with Sony Music, because Sony and I didn't have the same musical vision as I once had with Columbia Records. The song never was released as a single, but to this day I think it's a wonderful song and a testimony to Randy Goodrum's playing. The lyric of that song sounds like a girl's name, and it very well can be. It really is about music. It's about believing in the melody in the music.

"Open Arms."

One of the second writing sessions I had with Jonathan Cain was in my house. He showed up with an old Wurlitzer piano. We sat there and he played me some sketches, some ideas and some chords. We were just noodling around and then he played this melody, and I said, "What is that?" He said, "That is something I had written and played for John Waite when I was in the Babys, but he didn't like it." I said, "Too bad for him, and good for us because that is beautiful." That was the second song we wrote together.

"Send Her My Love."

This is one of the most cinematic songs I have had the pleasure of being involved in. Jonathan Cain came to me during a lyric session and said he wanted to write a song called "Send Her My Love." He said he loved that title. Everybody you know, when they break up, they don't want to call each other. But friends will stop you on the sidewalk and talk. Then you walk away and say, "Next time you see her, do me a favor and send her my love." He liked that. Not that you want to call, just "send her my love." I must admit that was just perfect. I have always envisioned some small café along the sidewalk with only two people per table, and me sitting with my ex-girlfriend. I envision what it would be like to send her my love in the future, because somewhere in my heart I always knew that we were not going to make it. If we are going to break up, then someday down the line I would want to be able to have the strength to tell somebody, "If you see her, send her my love." That's where all the small café stuff comes from.

Are you happy with the recording?

Between the opening drum part, Neal's lick, and Jonathan's playing, everything is musically poised for me to come in. It just sets up my vocal entrance beautifully. I come in and start singing against those changes. To this day.... I still love those changes.

You are doing the duet thing with Jonathan at one point and a duet with Neal at another.

And then I'm doing the duet at some point with them both because they are playing parts together, too. During the B section, "Calling out her name, I'm dreaming. Reflections of a face I'm seeing. It's her voice that keeps on haunting me," all of sudden it seems like the whole song is a dream. The track has a real dreamy quality to it. Neal had just gotten a Lexicon 480L. It was one of the most high-end echo units of its time that you could only find in a recording studio. He put one in his guitar rack and he adapted that to his sound. It gave it this huge across-the-Grand-Canyon dreamy feeling.

"Still They Ride"

"Still They Ride" is one of my favorite car songs. When I grew up in central San Joaquin Valley, there was a thickness in the summer night after a certain time of evening, when most of the people were gone and there were only a few still cruising Main Street. The town was so quiet that this thickness in the night had its own reality. That's where this song came from. The youth who still cruise at night still rule the night. There is something forever about it, and I love it for that. Jesse is a metaphor for a guy who won't give up the fantasy. It's probably a metaphor for me, but I love the name Jesse. "Jesse rides through the night under the Main Street light, riding slow. This old town ain't the same; now, nobody knows his name. Times have changed; still he rides. Traffic lights keeping time..." When cruising down Main Street at night, if you caught the right timing, you could watch the traffic lights go green and then the next block, green, and the next block, green in some kind of delayed rhythm. If you were caught in the right place in the wave of the green, you could cruise soulfully all the way through. "Traffic lights keeping time, leading the wild and restless through the night."

"When You Love a Woman."

Journey had been broken up for many years. We had gone through about as much as a band could musically and personally, and we'd put as many miles as a band ever could underneath our wheels. After a long break up, I thought it was time for us to get back together. The first person I called was Jonathan Cain. I asked, "What do you think about putting the band back together?" We talked, just the two of us first, in a café. Then he said, "We should get together with Neal and the three of us should have this conversation." We three got together. We were poised to tour and go out again. We got one of the best managers we could possibly find, Irving Azoff. He helped with putting the rest of the whole thing together. Unfortunately, that never happened because my left hip crashed during a hike while on break on the island after we had written, recorded, and mastered the new *Trial by Fire* CD. I had to start looking for surgeons to replace my hip. Somewhere along the way, impatience set in between the band and me, and they checked out another singer, which upset me terribly. They gave me an ultimatum, and I did not like that very much. So the next thing I knew, we were apart again and have been ever since May 8, 1998. "When You Love a Woman" not only became our first single from the *Trial by Fire* CD, but it was nominated that year for a Grammy. That became the epitome of our reunion success. We were good together.

Did the song feel fresh because it had been years between Journey songs?

I was so excited not only that we were together, but that we were working with Irving Azoff. There was something about him that gave me assurance that a lot of our business problems would be solved and I'd be able to let go and just be a singer/songwriter with the band again. I have a tendency to be concerned about a lot of things. I didn't want to get stretched out across all these areas. Irving would take care of all the details, and it felt so good to know that. So I was driving up to Jon's to write. After talking to Irving on the phone, I was feeling so free that I grabbed my cassette player and sang, "When You Love aa Woman." I sang the whole chorus melody. When I got up there we wrote it right on the spot and did the lyrics later. That's the testimony to what freedom of creativity can do when you are not locked up with outside concerns.

"Missing You."

I had heard this vocalist named Tim Miner, and I thought he had an incredible, emotional voice. I also heard that he wrote a lot of his stuff. I wanted to write with him. He came over to my place and we sat down, and "Missing You" was one of the quickest writing sessions I have ever been involved in. Because I had such respect for his voice, I think it helped me pull something out of myself I wouldn't otherwise have. The next thing I knew I was in Texas, where he lived at the time, and we were recording the track and with the Dallas Symphony.

But you were happy with the recording?

Of course, everything can be better. Everything I've ever done could be better. That's just the way it is!

You are comfortable letting these "children" go and grow on their own?

All these songs are like children. They've grown up and they've moved on. These songs have lives of their own at this point. I think this book is a testimony to the fact that these songs are classic in nature and they are locked into people's hearts. I know this because people stop me on the street and tell me so. This isn't my thinking; this is what they tell me. So I think these children, these songs, have grown up and they've made their statement, they're finally on their own, still strong and I'm oh so proud of them.

PHOTO: JOHN SCARPATI

Any Way You Want It

Words and Music by
Steve Perry and Neil Schon

G
D/F#
Em7
She loves to move, she loves to groove,
Ooh, then we touched, then we sang
N. C.
she loves the lov-in' things.
a - bout the lov-in' things.
G
D/F#
Ooh, all night,
Em7
all night, oh, ev - 'ry night.
NC
G
D/F#
Em7
N. C.
So hold tight, hold tight, ooh ba - by, hold tight.

G
Chorus
D/F#
Oh, she said, "An - y way you want it, that's
the way you need it, an - y way you want it."
Em7
N. C.
G
D/F#
Em7
She said, "An - y way you want it, that's the way you need it, an -
y way you want it."
NC
1. 2.
G
3.4. etc.
D.S. repeat chorus ad lib and fade
G
She said,"An-

A Brand New Start

Words and Music by
Steve Perry and David Pack

*Recorded a half step lower.

C
Am7
al - ways you. You were al - ways there. Just to
You held on for so man - y days. I know
C/F
Gsus4
G
stay with you, that would be my pray'r. And it's
you were hurt in so man - y ways. You
C
Am7
not like you did an - y - thing wrong. 'Cause
know I tried so man - y times. And
C/D
C/F
Gsus4
G
I was your sing - er and you were my song.
girl, I'm so sor - ry I made you cry.

C/D
G/A
3fr
C/D
G/A
3fr
Shades of for - ev - er that turn in - to gray.
Play 1st time only
C/D
G/A
3fr
Fmaj7
Gsus4
G
You're my to - mor - row that I've lost to - day.
Play 2nd time only
Fmaj7
Gsus4
G
C
I've lost to - day.
You tried to reach some - thing
G/B
Am
C/G
you could not touch.
May - be there in the end we'll find we

D7/F#
Fmaj7
Em7
Am7
both cared too much.
Here's where our blue skies
Fmaj7
E7sus4
E
sad - ly turn dark.
We were
Am7
D/F#
To Coda
Fmaj7
Gsus4
G
al - most a part of a brand - new
(A part.)
1.
C
F/C
G/C
C
Am7
F/A
G/A
3fr
Gsus4
G
start.

2.
C
B♭sus2
start. A bro - ken man takes
(Start.) (Bro - ken man.)
F/A
B♭sus2
F/A
one more fall. An - oth - er choice that makes no sense at
(One more fall.)
C
B♭sus2
all. But it's just like me to
(Just like me.)
F
B♭sus2
F/A
run a - way and nev - er find the words I need to
(Run a - way.)

Gsus4
Gsus4/F
C/E
D7sus4
D.S. al Coda
say.
(What I need to say.)
Woh.
Coda
Fmaj7
Gsus4
G
Am7
D7/F♯
brand - new start,
of a
(Of a brand...)
(Start.)
Fmaj7
Gsus4
G
Fmaj7
Am7
brand - new start.
(Of a brand...)
(Start.)
Dm7add4
3fr
B♭
Cadd2
rit.

Don't Fight It

Words and Music by
Steve Perry, Dean Pitchford
and Kenny Loggins

G D C G D
brew__ will do,__ but there's times ___ you'll wind up feel - in' so ___ fine.
scrap - in' the sky._ Is ev - 'ry - bod - y read - y to move?
A G D A
Some wom - en seem to have a knack._ They'll turn __ you on and
There's times you wan - na shake your - self.___ There's nights_ you wan - na
G D A G D
leave you flat. You nev - er can tell who's play - in' for keeps,_ so tell ____
yell for help. You can't fly when you're stand - ing still.___ There's noth -
C G D C
— me what's hold - ing you back. I know ______ your heart can
ing wrong with rais - ing some hell. To - night, ______ we're gon - na

G
D
A
take it.
raise it!
Don't fight it, don't fight it,
G
D
don't fight it. It-'ll do your heart so good. Don't fight it,
A
G
don't fight it, don't fight it. It-'ll do your heart so good.
D
A
1.
Bm
Don't fight it, don't fight it, don't fight it. It-'ll

G
D
on - ly do you good.
2. G
Bm
don't fight it. It - 'll do your heart so. Do what ma - ma do,
D
Bm
do what dad - dy do. When you gon - na make up your mind? You can run, but
G
A
D. S. 𝄋 and fade
love will find you. Read - y or not, here it comes.

Don't Stop Believin'

Words and Music by
Steve Perry, Neal Schon
and Jonathan Cain

C♯m7
4fr
A
liv - in' in a lone - ly world.
born and raised in south De - troit.
E
B
She took the mid - night train go - in'
He took the mid - night train go - in'
G♯m
4fr
1.
A
2.
A
an - y - where.
an - y - where.
E
B
C♯m7
4fr

A
E
B
G♯m
4fr
A
E
B
A sing - er in a smok - y room.
C♯m7
4fr
A
E
The smell of wine and cheap per - fume.
For a smile they can

B
G#m
4fr
A
share the night. It goes on and on and on and on.
3
cresc.
B/A
A
B/A
E/A
B/E
E
Stran - gers wait - ing up and down the
Street - light peo - ple, liv - ing just to
f
B/E
E
B/A
A
1.
B/A
E/A
boul - e - vard, their shad - ows search - ing in the night.
find e - mo - tion, hid - ing
B/E
E
B/E
E
2.
B/A
E/A
some - where in the night.

B E B E A
To Coda
E
B C#m7 A
E B C#m7
Work - in' hard to get my fill. Ev - 'ry - bod - y
A E B
wants a thrill. Pay - in' an - y - thing to roll the dice just

G#m
4fr
A
one more time.
E
B
C#m7
4fr
3
Some will win, some will lose, some were born to
A
E
B
sing the blues. Oh, the mov-ie nev-er ends; it goes
G#m
4fr
A
D.S. (with repeat) al Coda
on and on and on and on.

Coda
E
B
C♯m7
4fr
A
E
B
G♯m
4fr
A
E
B
C♯m7
4fr
Don't stop be - liev - in'.
Hold on to the
A
E
B
feel - in', street - light peo - ple.

G♯m
4fr
A
E
Don't stop be -
B
C♯m7
4fr
liev - ing.
Hold on,
A
E
street - light
B
G♯m
4fr
A
Repeat and fade
peo - ple.
3
3

Faithfully

Words and Music by
Jonathan Cain

Rest - less hearts sleep a -
Through space and time al - ways an -
G♯m
4fr
E
lone to - night, send - in' all my love a - long the
oth - er show. Won - d'ring where I am; lost with -
B/F♯
F♯
E
G♯m
4fr
wire. They say that the road ain't no place to start a fam
out you. And be - ing a - part ain't eas - y on this
B
Emaj7
G♯m
4fr
- 'ly. Right down the line it's been you and me.
love af - fair; two strang - ers learn to fall in love a - gain.

B
E
And lov - in' a mu - sic man ain't al - ways what it's
I get the joy of re - dis -
B
F♯
D♯m
6fr
s'pposed to be.
cov - 'ring you.
Oh girl, you stand by
F♯
C♯m
4fr
3
me.
I'm for - ev - er yours,
E
B
faith - ful - ly.
mp

G♯m
4fr
B/F♯
1
E
2.
E
Cir - cus
B
G♯m
4fr
1. Oh,
2.-5. (Vocal ad lib.)
oh,
f
B/F♯
1-4
E
5
E
oh.

Foolish Heart

Words and Music by
Steve Perry and Randy Goodrum

*Recorded a half step lower.

C7 C9 Am7 Am7add4 Am7 D7sus4 D7
pass - ing hour, some - one, some - how will be there
F/G Fmaj9 G/F Fadd9 G/F
read - y to share. I need a love that's strong. I'm so
Feel - ing that feel - ing a - gain. I'm
Fmaj9 G/F Fadd9 G/F C7 C9
ti - red of be - ing a - lone. But will my lone - ly heart
play - ing a game I can't win. Love's knock - ing on the door of my
Am7 Am7add4 Am7 D7sus4 D7 F/G
play the part of the fool a - gain be - fore I be - gin?
heart once more. Think I'll let her in be - fore I be - gin.
Fool - ish heart,

Fsus2
G/B
C
Fmaj9
3fr
hear me call - ing. Stop be - fore you start
G/B
C
Fsus2
G/B
C
G/B
fall - ing. Fool - ish heart heed my warn - ing. You've been
1.
Am7
D7sus4
D7
F/G
Fmaj9
3fr
G/F
wrong be - fore; don't be wrong an - y - more.
F
G/F
Fmaj9
3fr
G/F
F
G/F

2.
Am7
D7sus4
D7
F/G
Fmaj9
3fr
wrong be - fore; don't be wrong an - y - more. Fool - ish heart.
G/B
C
Fmaj9
3fr
G/B
C
Fool - ish, fool - ish heart.
Fmaj9
3fr
G/B
C
G/B
Am7
D7sus4
D7
You've been wrong be - fore.
F/G
N.C.
mp

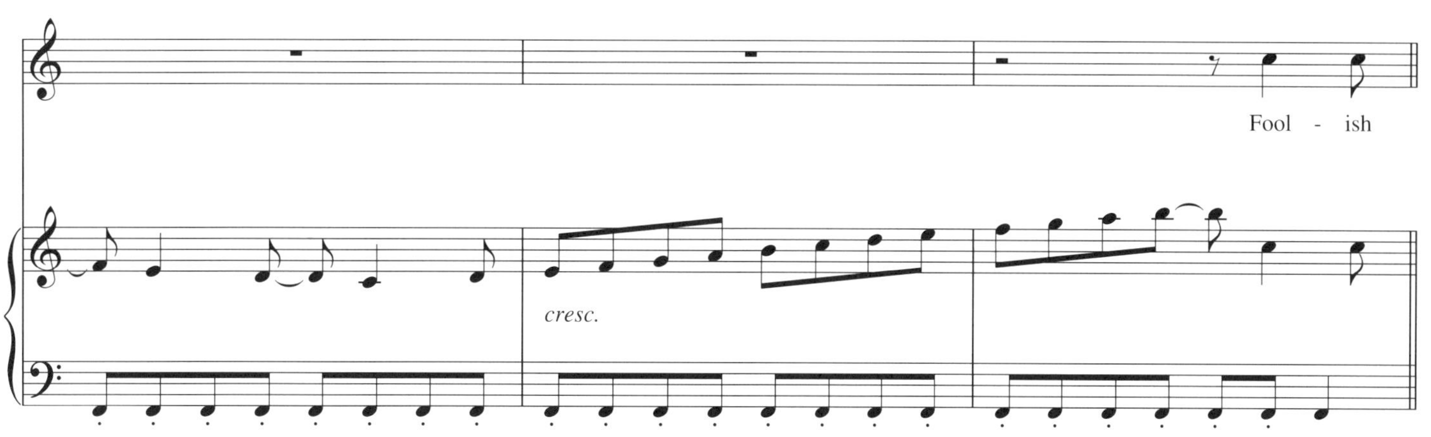

Fool - ish
cresc.

Fmaj9
G/B
C
Fmaj9
3fr
heart, hear me call - ing. Stop be - fore you start
mf

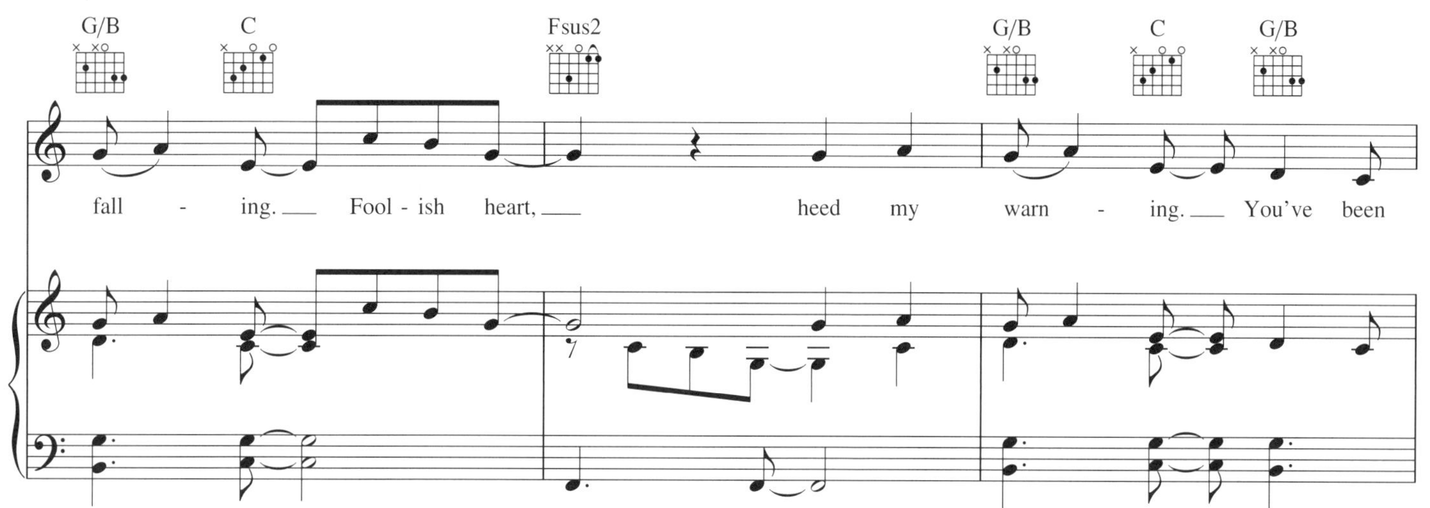

G/B
C
Fsus2
G/B
C
G/B
fall - ing. Fool - ish heart, heed my warn - ing. You've been

Am7
D7sus4
D7
F/G
Fsus2
wrong be - fore; don't be wrong an - y - more. Fool - ish heart.
G/B
C
Fmaj9
3fr
G/B
C
Fsus2
Oh, fool - ish, fool - ish heart.
G/B
C
G/B
Am7
D7sus4
D7
F/G
You've been wrong be - fore.
Repeat and fade
Fsus2
G/B
C
Fmaj9
3fr
G/B
C
Vocal ad lib...

Good Morning Girl

Words and Music by
Steve Perry and Matt Schon

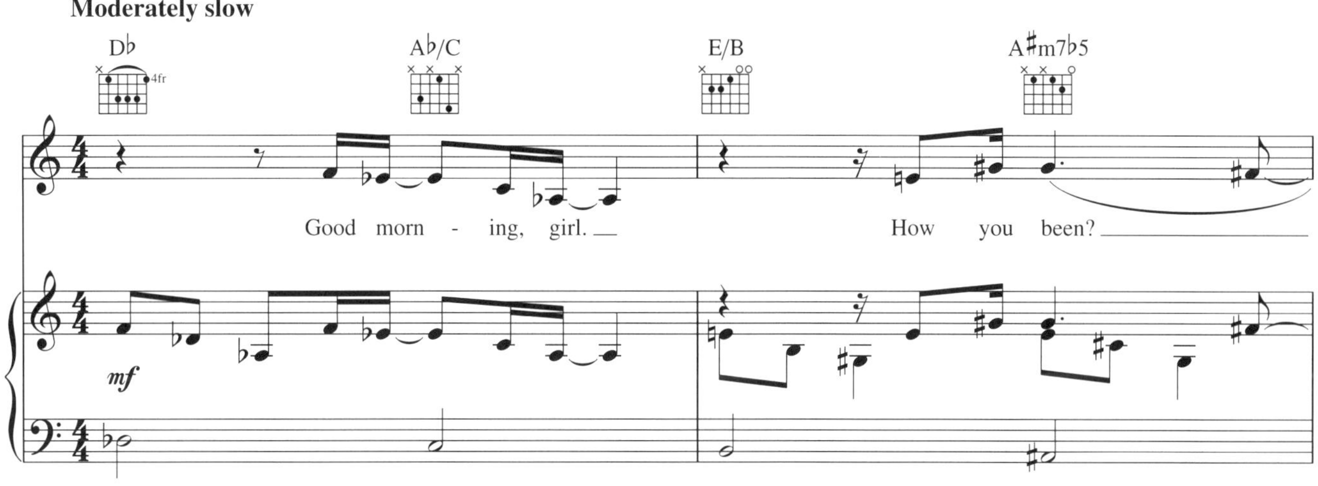

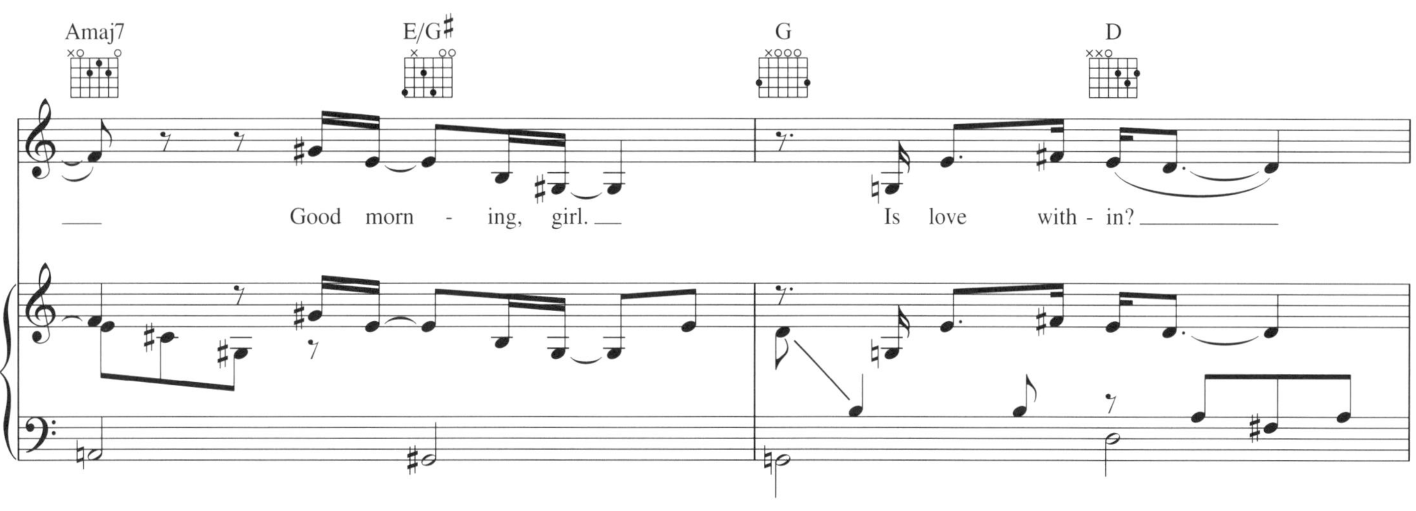

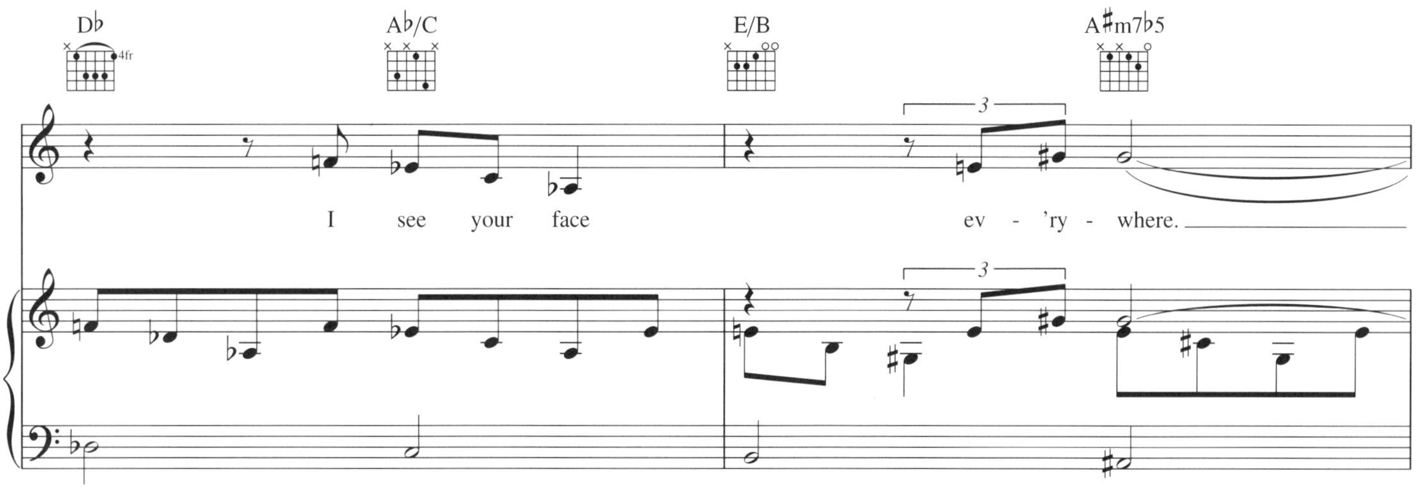

Amaj7
E/G♯
G
D
I see your smile, your gold - en hair.
C
G/B
B♭
F/A
I see your eyes shin - in' through.
A♭
E♭/G
B♭7sus4/F
G5
Those gen - tle eyes, sil - ver blue.
D♭
A♭/C
E/B
A♯m7♭5
Good morn - ing, girl. How you been?

Amaj7
E/G♯
G
D
Good morn - ing, girl.
Is love with - in?
A/C♯
C
G/B
Good morn - ing, girl.
It's been long.
B♭
F/A
A♭
4fr
E♭
Good morn - ing, girl.
To you, this song.
B♭/D
D♭
4fr
A♭/C
I sing it, girl,
from the heart.

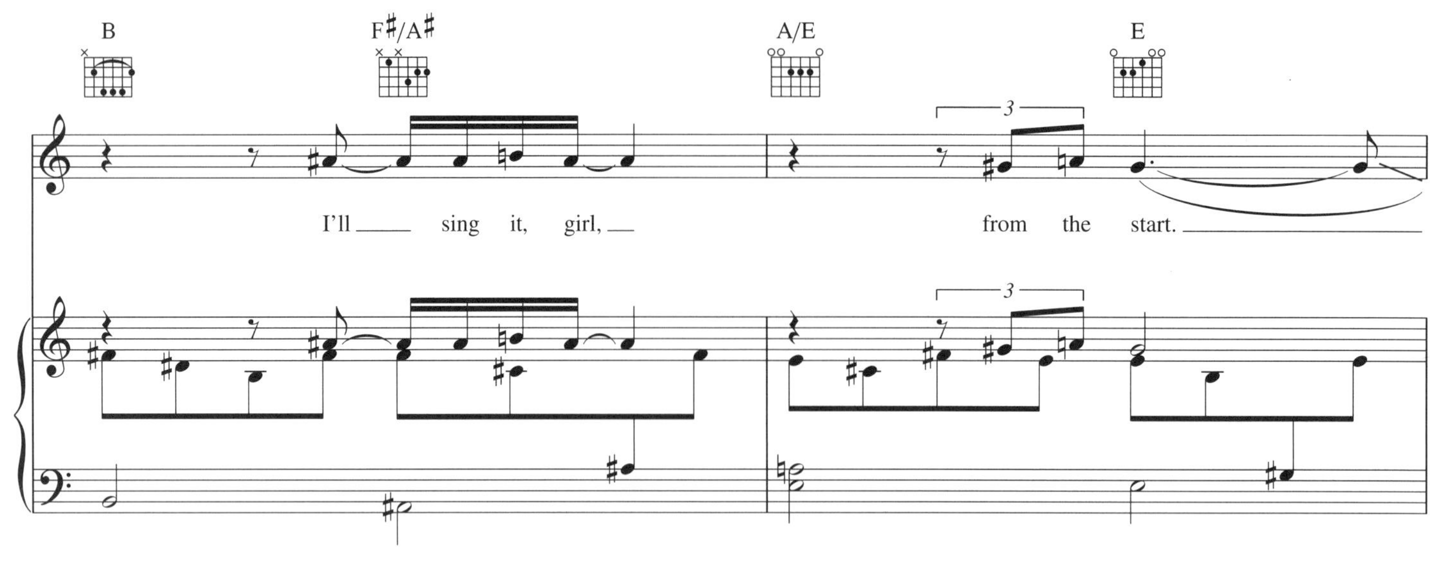
B
F♯/A♯
A/E
E
I'll sing it, girl,
from the start.

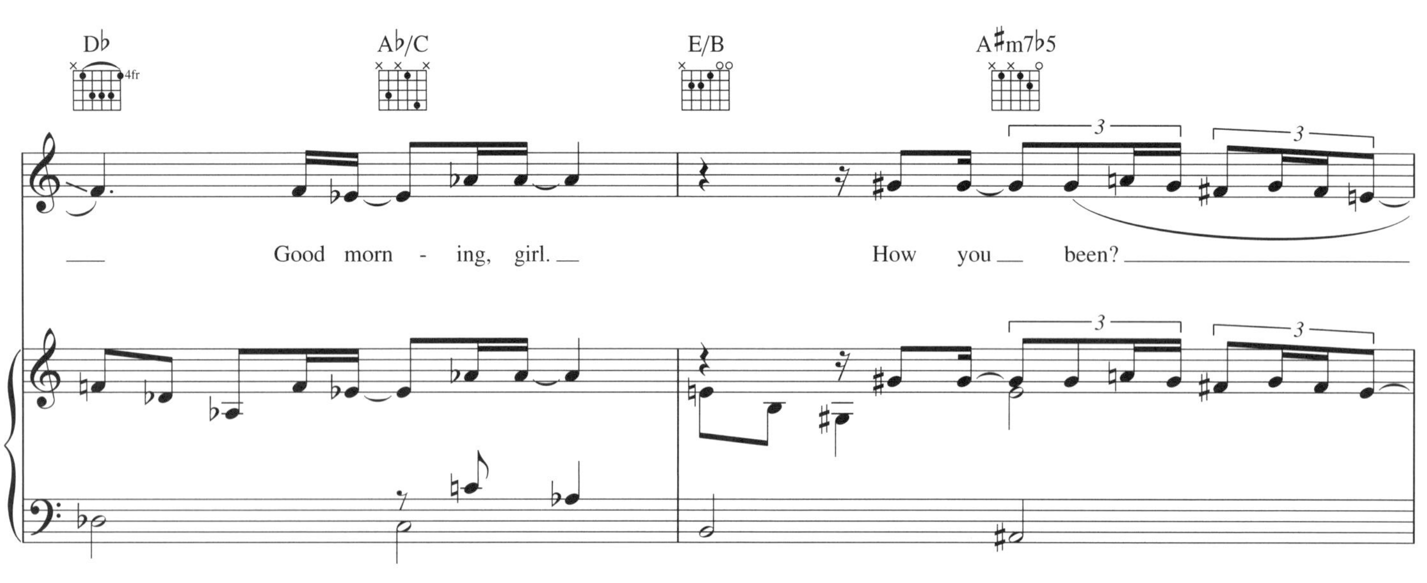
D♭
4fr
A♭/C
E/B
A♯m7♭5
Good morn - ing, girl.
How you been?

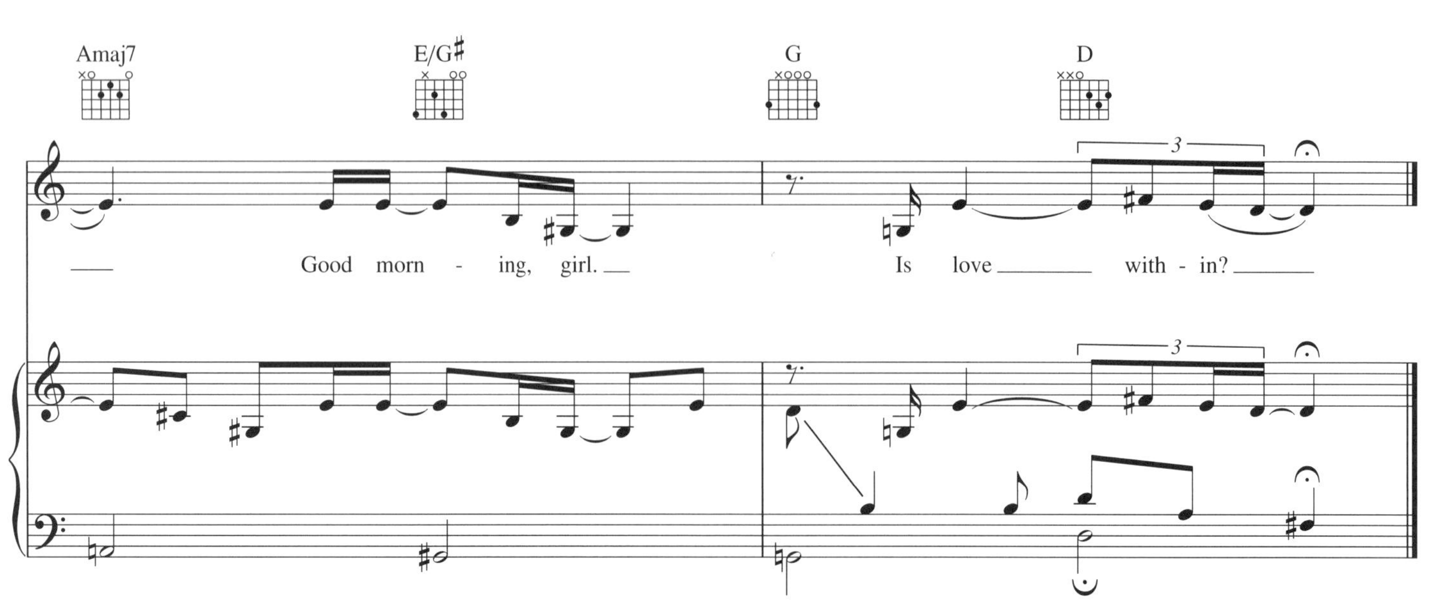
Amaj7
E/G♯
G
D
Good morn - ing, girl.
Is love with - in?

Lights

Words and Music by
Steve Perry and Neal Schon

C
Bm
C
To Coda
city - y,
oh, oh, oh,
oh,
oh, oh,
cit - y
by
the
bay
oh
oh
1
2, 3
D
D
Bm
G
oh.
oh.
It's sad,
oh,
there's been
Guitar solo
mf
D
Bm
G
morn - ings out on the road with - out you, with - out your
D
A
F♯/A♯
Bm
G
4fr
charms,
oh, oh, oh,
my, my,

D
Bm
C
my, my, my, my, oh, oh,

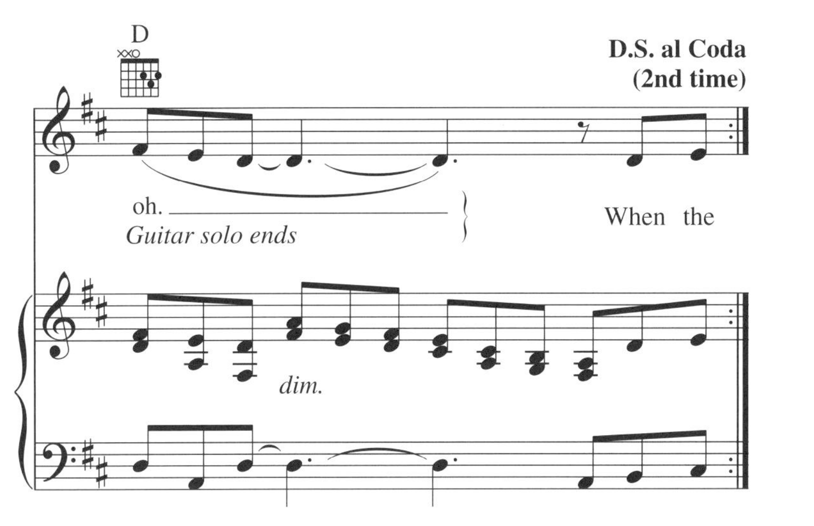
D
D.S. al Coda
(2nd time)
oh.
Guitar solo ends
When the
dim.

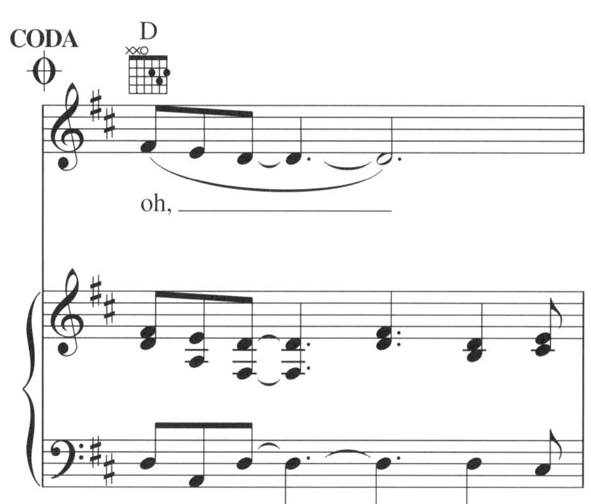
CODA
D
oh,

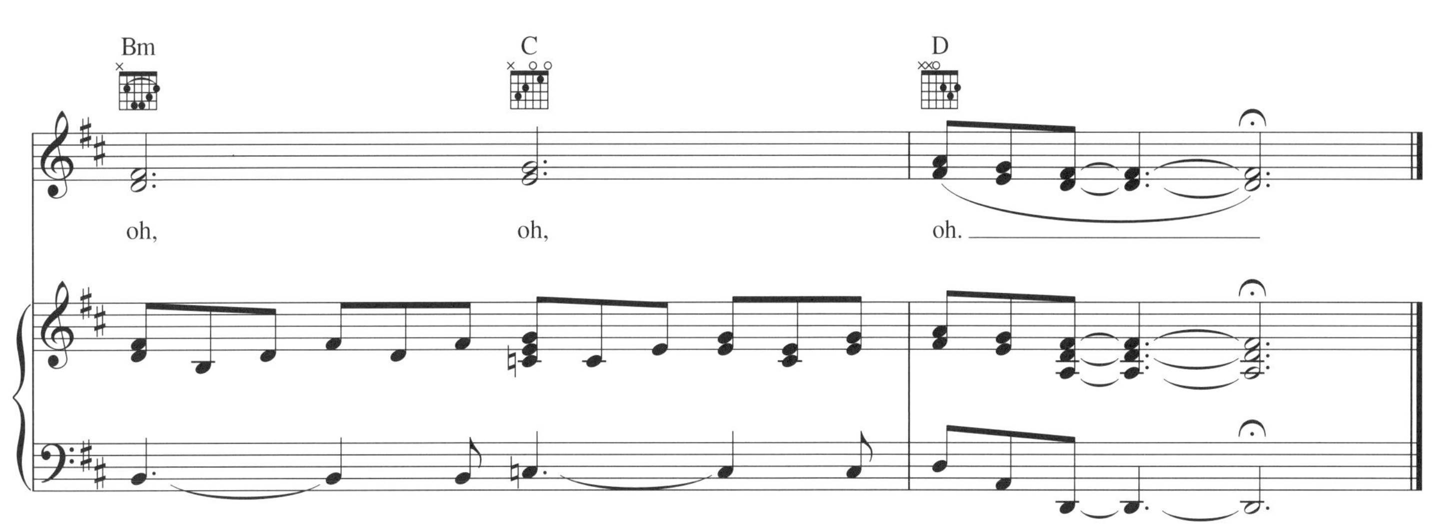
Bm
C
D
oh, oh, oh.

Lovin', Touchin', Squeezin'

Words and Music by
Steve Perry

A
E
G
lov - in' touch-in' squeez - in' each
lov - in' touch-in' squeez - in' each
1
G
A
oth - er.
When I'm a -
2.3.
G
A
F#m
oth - er.
Chorus:
You're tear - in' me a - part
He's tear - in' you a - part
A
F#m
To Coda
ev - er - y, ev - er - y day you're tear-in' me a - part
ev - er - y, ev - er - y day he's tear-in' you a - part

A
F♯m
Oh what can I say? You're tear - in' me a - part.
cresc.
G
E
D
D.S. al Coda
f
Coda
A
F♯m
G
Oh girl what can you say? 'Cause he's lov - in', touch - in' an -
cresc.
f
A
F♯m
G
oth - er. Now it's your turn girl to cry.

3rd Verse:

It won't be long, yes
Till you're alone, when your lover,
Oh, he hasn't come home
'Cause he's lovin' oo, he's touchin', he's squeezin' another.
(To Chorus:)

Melody

Words and Music by
Steve Perry and Randy Goodrum

G/B
A♭/C
A/C♯
B♭/D
G/B
A♭/C
In my dreams, telling me you're not illusion. You belong to me.
Hold me now, tell me all the answers that my heart will ever seek.
A/C♯
B♭/D
B♭/D
C♭/E♭
C/E
D♭/F
D/F♯
E♭/G
G
A♭
Bm7sus4
Cm7sus4
Mel - o - dy, I be - lieve in you.
*(Mel - o - dy.)
*1st time, bkgd. vocal tacet (this bar only)
Bm7
Cm7
G
A♭
Asus4
B♭sus4
Mel - o - dy in my heart.
(Mel - o - dy.)

D/F#
G
E♭/G
A♭
Mel - o - dy, I still
(Mel - o - dy.)
Bm7sus4
Bm7
Em7
D/F#
Cm7sus4
Cm7
Fm7
E♭/G
reach for you. Hold me, Mel - o - dy.
G
Asus4
A
Em7
D/F#
To Coda
A♭
B♭sus4
B♭
Fm7
E♭/G
Hold me, Mel - o - dy.
1.
2.
G
G
Asus4
A♭
A♭
B♭sus4

G/B
A♭/C
A/C♯
B♭/D
G/B
A♭/C
A/C♯
B♭/D
B♭/D
C♭/E♭
C/E
D♭/F
D/F♯
E♭/G
D.S. al Coda
8va
Coda
G
A♭
Asus4
B♭sus4
G
A♭
8va
Repeat and fade
(8va)

Missing You

Words and Music by
Steve Perry and Tim Miner

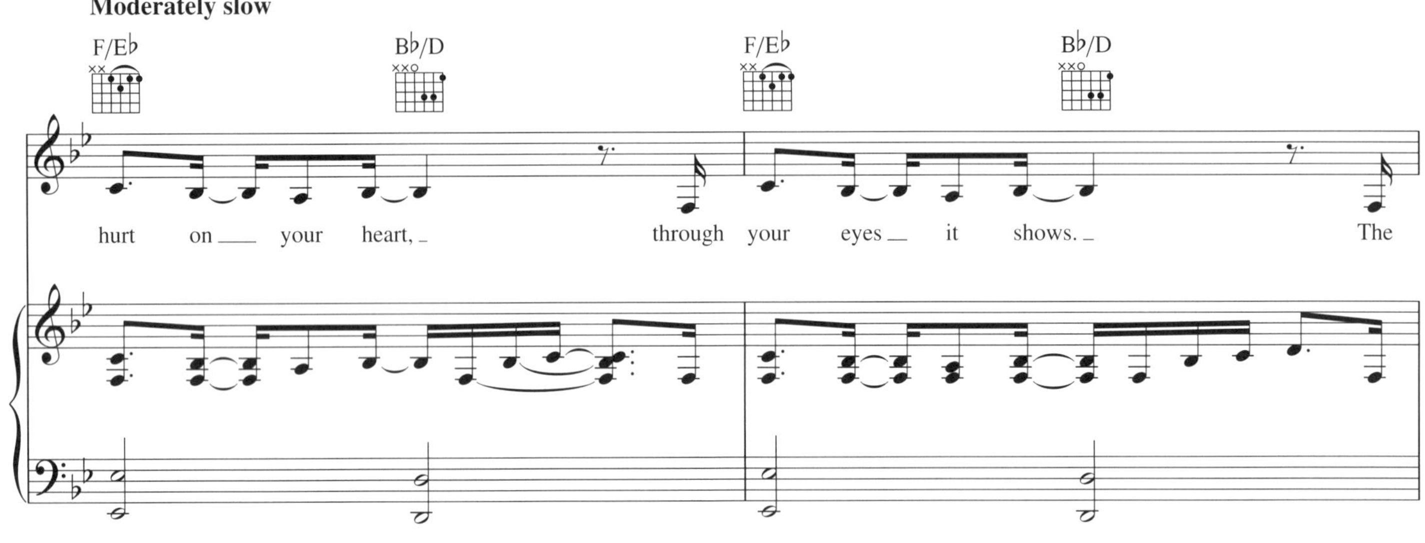

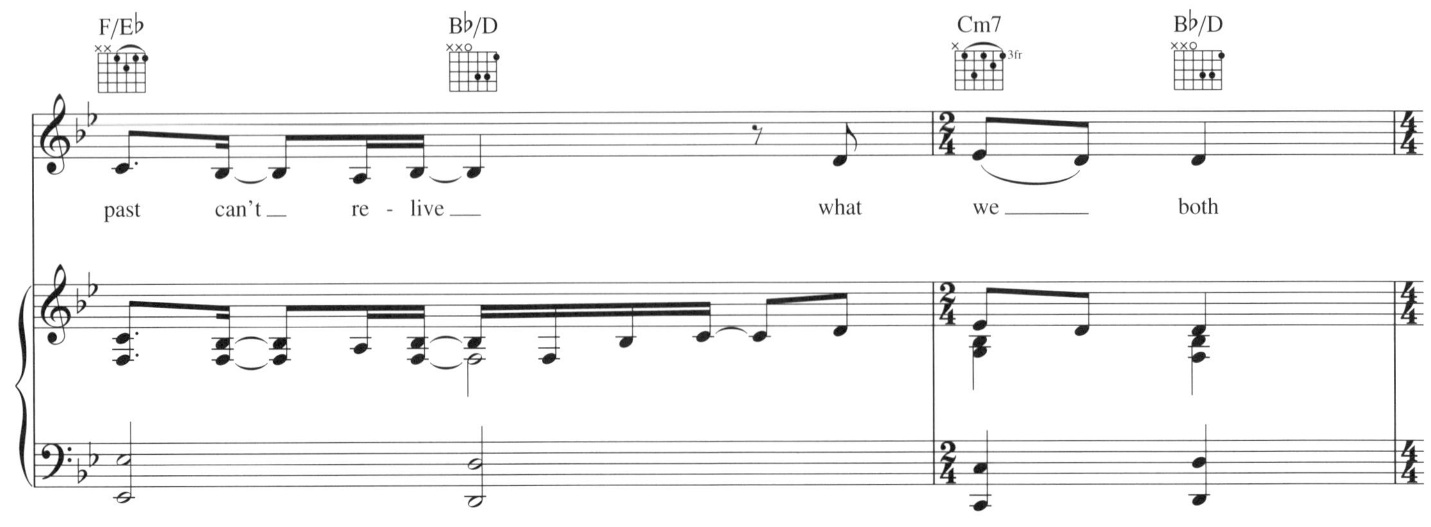

Fsus4
F
F/E♭
B♭/D
know.
Still I re - mem - ber
F/E♭
B♭/D
F/E♭
B♭/D
things I'll nev - er miss.
Mem - 'ries sur - round me, won't
Cm7
B♭/D
Fsus4
F
let me for - get.
I was so
E♭maj9
Gm7
E♭maj9
Gm7
wrong.
The se - cret's not worth keep - ing. I

Cm7
3fr
Gm7
3fr
F/A
F
had no faith that you would still be - lieve.
No,
E♭maj9
Gm7
3fr
E♭maj9
Gm7
3fr
now
my heart's in your keep - ing.
Cm7
3fr
B♭/D
Fsus4
F
Here I am
miss - ing you,
Fsus4/E♭
Gm
3fr
F/A
B♭
(miss - ing you).

F/E♭
B♭/D
F/E♭
B♭/D
Feel - ing the dark stares from my wall, your
F/E♭
B♭/D
Cm7
B♭/D
3fr
eyes in your pic - ture won't let me
Fsus4
F
F/E♭
B♭/D
go. If I could re - mem - ber how
F/E♭
B♭/D
F/E♭
B♭/D
you felt the pain, the king of pre - tend - ers a -

Cm7
B♭/D
Fsus4
F7
3fr
lone in shame. I was so
E♭maj9
Gm7
E♭maj9
Gm7
wrong. The se - cret's not worth keep - ing. I
Cm7
Gm7
F/A
F
had no faith that you would still be - lieve. No,
E♭maj9
Gm7
E♭maj9
Gm7
now my heart's in your keep - ing.

Cm7
B♭/D
Fsus4
F
B♭/F
Here I am. Oh,
Cm7
B♭/D
Fsus4/E♭
here I am
(miss - ing you),
N.C.
B♭/D
Gm7
miss - ing you.
Cm7
Fsus4
F/A
Gm
F/A
B♭
Woh, oh, I'm
(miss - ing you).
You were

E♭maj9
Dm7
Gm7
there, now I'm here. You gave
Cm7
Fsus4
F/A
Gm7
F/A
B♭
much more than I did. I save what I had to give. If I
E♭maj9
Dm7
Gm7
could, you know I, I would.
Cm7
Fsus4
F7/A
Gm
F/A
B♭
I'd make it up to you. In - stead I'm In the
(miss - ing you).

E♭maj9
Dm7
Gm7
3fr
place you used to be,
you were
Cm7
Fsus4
F/A
Gm7
F/A
B♭
3
ly - ing next to me.
Oh, I'm
E♭maj9
B♭/D
Gm7
miss - ing you.
Cm7
Fsus4
F/A
Gm7
F/A
B♭
Woh, oh, I'm
Oh,
ooh.
(miss - ing you).
rit.

Oh Sherrie

Words and Music by
Steve Perry, Randy Goodrum,
Bill Cuomo and Craig Krampf

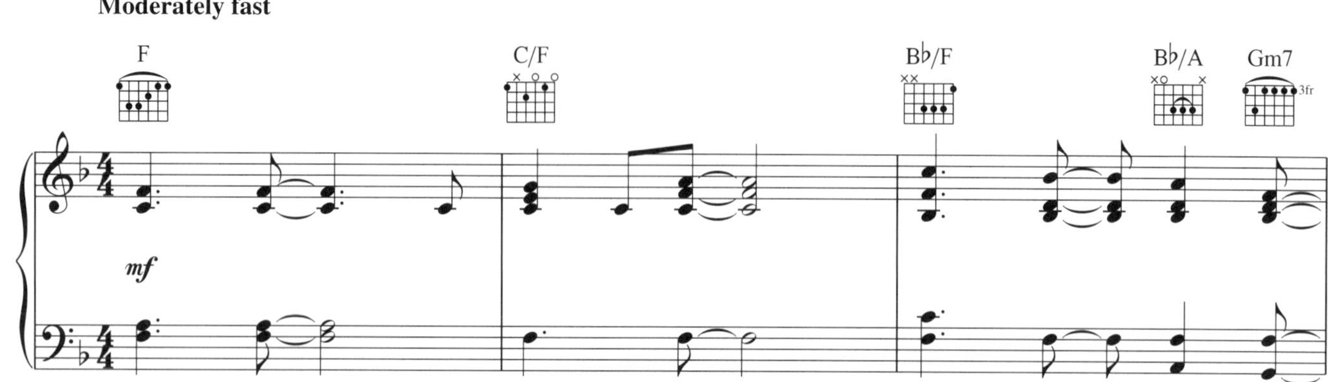

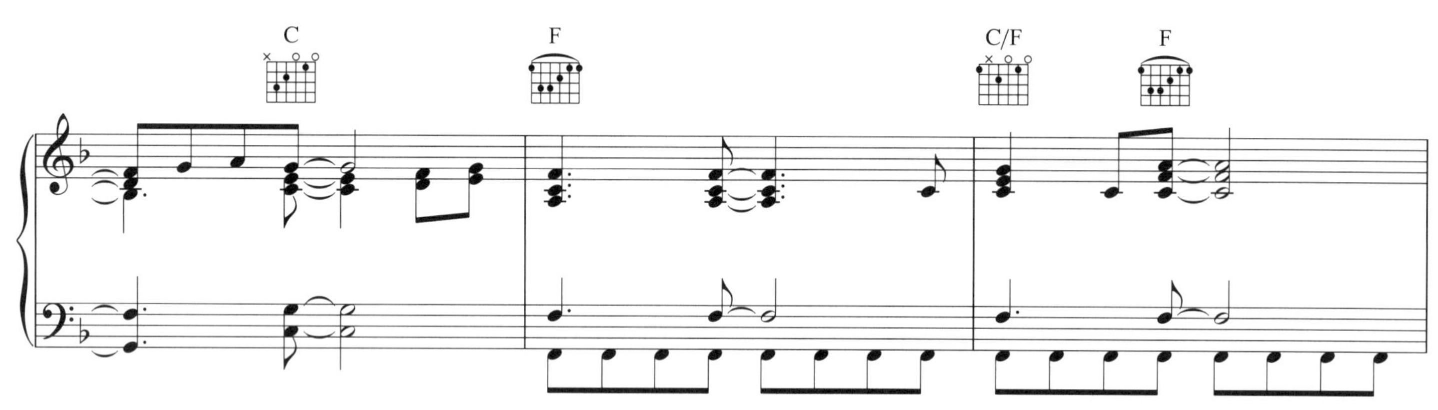

Tacet
gone, knowing how I made you feel. And I should-'ve been
Bb/D
C/D
Dm
gone after all your words of steel.
Bb
F/C
C
Oh, I must-'ve been a dreamer
(Must-'ve been a dreamer,
Bb
F/C
C
And I must-'ve been someone else.
no,
Someone else.)

B♭
F/C
C
And we should-'ve been o - ver.
(O - ver by now.)
F
C/F
F
A♭/F
E♭/F
Oh Sher - rie, our love holds on,
(Hold - in' on.)
Gm/F
F
C/F
F
holds on. Oh Sher - rie, our love
(Hold - in' on.)
A♭/F
E♭/F
Gm/C
F
holds on, holds on. But I wan - na let

Dm
B♭/D
C/D
Dm
go.
You'll go on
hurt - in' me.
B♭/D
C/D
You'd be bet - ter off a - lone
if I'm not who you
Dm
Dm/C
B♭
thought I'd be.
But you know that there's a
F/C
C
B♭
fe - ver,
(Know that there's a fe - ver, no,
oh, that you'll nev - er find

F/C
C
B♭
F/C
no - where else.
Can't you feel it burn - ing on and on?
no - where else.)
(No - where else.
On and on.)
F
C/F
F
A♭/F
E♭/F
3fr
Oh, Sher - rie, our love holds on,
(Hold - in' on.)
Gm/F
F
C/F
F
holds on.
Oh Sher - rie, our love
(Hold - in' on.)
A♭/F
E♭/F
3fr
Gm/F
F
F
holds on,
holds on.

C/F
F
B♭sus2
Gm7
3fr
Csus4
Oh, Sher - rie.
F
C/F
F
A♭/F
3fr
E♭/F
Gm/F
F
A♭/F
3fr
E♭/F
Gm/F
F
Dm
B♭/D
C/D
But I should - 've been gone
long a - go,

Dm
far a - way.
And you should - 've been gone.
B♭/D
C/D
Dm
F
Now I know just why you stay.
Oh Sher - rie,
(Hold - in' on.)
C/F
F
A♭/F
E♭/F
Gm/F
F
our love holds on, holds on.
F
C/F
F
A♭/F
E♭/F
Oh Sher - rie, our love holds on,
(Hold - in' on.)

1.
2.
Gm/F
F
Gm/F
F
holds on.
holds on.
C/F
F
A♭/F
E♭/F
Gm/F
F
Hold on.
Oh Sher - rie.
A♭/F
E♭/F
Gm/F
F
F
C/F
F
B♭/F
B♭/A
Gm7
C
F
C/F
F
A♭/F
E♭/F
Gm/F
F
rit.

Open Arms

Words and Music by Steve Perry
and Jonathan Cain

G/B
Bm
A
G
cere. How could our love be so blind? We
near; how much I want - ed you home. But
Em
Bm
A/C♯
D
sailed on to - geth - er; we drift - ed a - part. And here you
now that you've come back, turned night in - to day, I
mf
A
G
A/G
G
A/G
Dadd2
are by my side.
need you to stay.
So now I come to
cresc.
f
D
Dsus9/F♯
D/F♯
G
C9
you with o - pen arms; noth - ing to hide, be - lieve what I

Dadd2
D
Dsus9/F♯
D/F♯
G
say. So here I am with o - pen arms, hop - ing you'll
C9
To Coda
D
A/C♯
see what your love means to me; o - pen arms.
dim.
mp
G/B
Bm
A
G
D.S. al Coda
Coda
D
arms.
mp
D/C
G/B
B♭/C
D
rit. e dim.
p

Patiently

Words and Music by
Steve Perry and Neal Schon

C
G/B
Gm/B♭
A7
for your song in - side of me.
for your lights to shine on me.
To Coda
Dm
Dm/C♯
Dm/C
G/B
This we bring to you.
This we bring to
C
G/B
Am
Em/G
In the shad - ow of love, time goes by,
D/F♯
Fmaj7
leav - ing me help - less.

C
G/B
Am
Em/G
Just to reach and try to live my life;
D/F♯
Fmaj7
these are my rea - sons.
C
G/B
Gm/B♭
A7
So here we stand so pa - tient - ly
Dm
Dm/C♯
Dm/C
G/B
for your song in - side of me,
3
3

C
G/B
Gm/B♭
A7
for your lights to shine on me.
Dm
Dm/C♯
Dm/C
G/B
This we bring to you.
C
G/B
Am
Am/G
D/F♯
Fmaj7
C
G/B
Am
Am/G
D/F♯
Fmaj7
C
One,
f

G/B
Am
Am/G
D/F♯
Fmaj7
C
one in a mil - lion.
Oh,
oh,
oh,
oh,
oh,
oh,
oh.

G/B
Am
Am/G
D/F♯
Fmaj7
C
3
G/B
Am
Am/G
D/F♯
Fmaj7
Em
mf
Fmaj7
D.S. al Coda
Coda
Dm/C
G/B
you.
rit.

Send Her My Love

Em9
C
a sad ca - fe; how it hurt
Em7
Bm7
C
so bad to see her cry.
I did- n't
Em
Bm7sus
Bm7
Chorus:
Em
want to say good - bye.
Send her my
mf
sfz
mf
Dadd9/F♯
C
Am(add9)
Em
love; mem - o-ries re - main.
Send her my love;

Dadd9/F♯
C
Amadd9
ros - es nev - er fade.
Em
1. Dadd9/F♯
Cadd9
3
Send her my love.
cresc.
f
sfz
D.S.
2. Dadd9/F♯
Cmaj7
love.
Call - in' out her name,
f
Em
I'm dream - in' re - flec - tions of a face I'm see - in'.

C
Bm7
It's her voice that keeps on haunt - ing me.
Em
Dadd9/F♯
C
1.2.3.
Am
Instrumental Solo ad lib.
4.
Am
Em
Dadd9/F♯
Send her, send her my love;
f
C
Amadd9
Em
ros - es nev - er fade.

Verse 2:
The same hotel, the same old room;
I'm on the road again.
She needed so much more
Than I could give.
We knew our love could not pretend.
Broken hearts can always mend.

(To chorus:)

Still They Ride

Words and Music by
Steve Perry, Neal Schon
and Jonathan Cain

Verse 3:
Traffic lights keepin' time;
Leading the wild and restless
Through the night.

Verse 4:
Spinning 'round, in a spell;
It's hard to leave this carousel.
'Round and 'round and 'round and 'round.

Stone in Love

Words and Music by
Steve Perry, Neal Schon
and Jonathan Cain

Csus2 Csus2/E Csus2 G/B G5 G/B Csus2
best times, most of all.
clo - ver we'd go 'round.
In the heat with a
D5 D/F♯ D5 Csus2 Csus2/E Csus2 G/B
blue jean girl.
Burn - in' love comes once in a life - time.
G5 G/B Csus2 D5 D/F♯ D5 Csus2 Csus2/E Csus2
She found me sing - ing by the rail - road track.
Oh, the mem - 'ries nev - er fade a - way.
Took me home; we
Gold - en girl, I'll
G/B D5 C5
danced by the moon - light.
keep you for - ev - er.
Those sum - mer nights are call - in'.

G5
C
G5
D5
Stone in love.
Can't help my-self,
To Coda
C5
G
I'm fall-in'.
Stone in love.
G/B
Csus2
D5
D/F♯
D5
Csus2
Csus2/E
Csus2
G/B
G5
G/B
Csus2
D5
D/F♯
D5
D.S. al Coda
Csus2
Csus2/E
Csus2
G/B

Coda
G
E♭/G
F/G
G
E♭/G
B♭5/G
F/G
G5
E♭/G
F/G
G5
E♭/G
B♭/G
F/G
G
Repeat and fade
E♭/G
Stone in love.

Wheel in the Sky

Words and Music by Robert Fleischman,
Neal Schon and Diane Valory

have - n't been home in a year or more.
got to make it be - fore too long
C
B♭
I hope she holds on a lit - tle
Ooo I can't take this ver - y much
Dm
long - er.
long - er.
Sent a let - ter on a long sum - mer day
I'm stand - in' in the sleet and rain.

made of sil - ver not of clay
Don't think I'll nev - er gon - na make it home a - gain.
C
B♭
ooo I've been run - nin' down this dust -
The morn - in' sun is ris - in'
Dm
- y road.
it's kiss - in' the day.
Ooo the
Dm
F
C
wheel in the sky keeps on turn - in' I
f

Dm
F
C
don't know where I'll be to - mor - row.
Dm
F
C
(1.,2.) Wheel in the sky keeps on turn - in'
(3.) Wheel in the sky keeps me yearn - in'
G/B
C
Gm/B♭
To Coda
whoa.
1
Dm

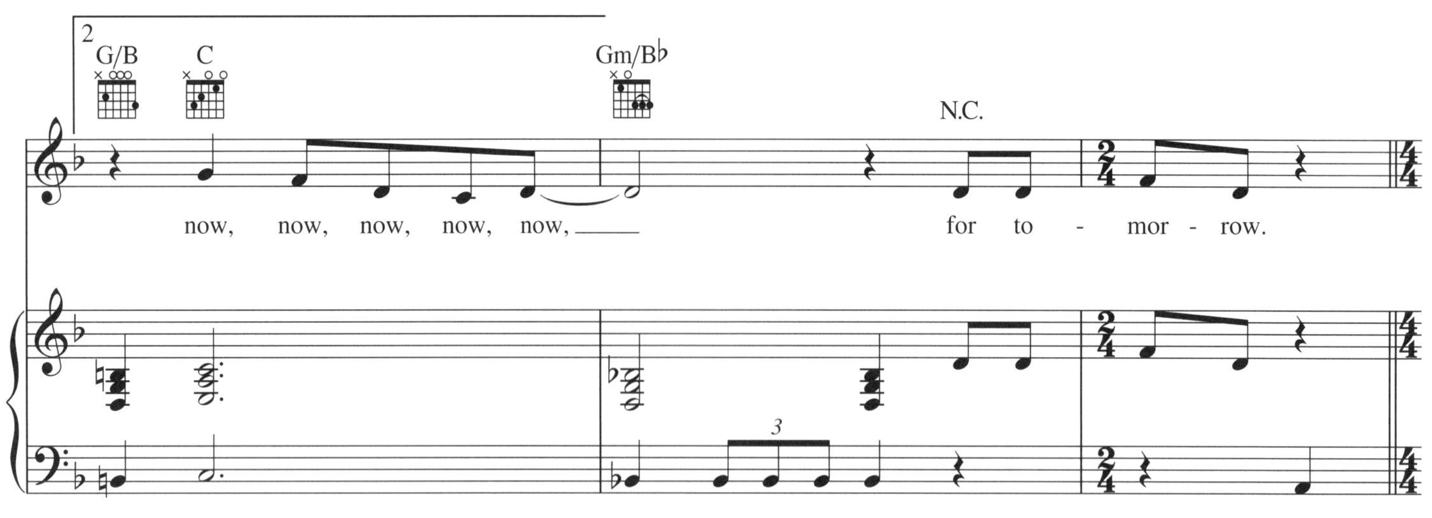
2
G/B
C
Gm/B♭
N.C.
now, now, now, now, now,
for to - mor - row.

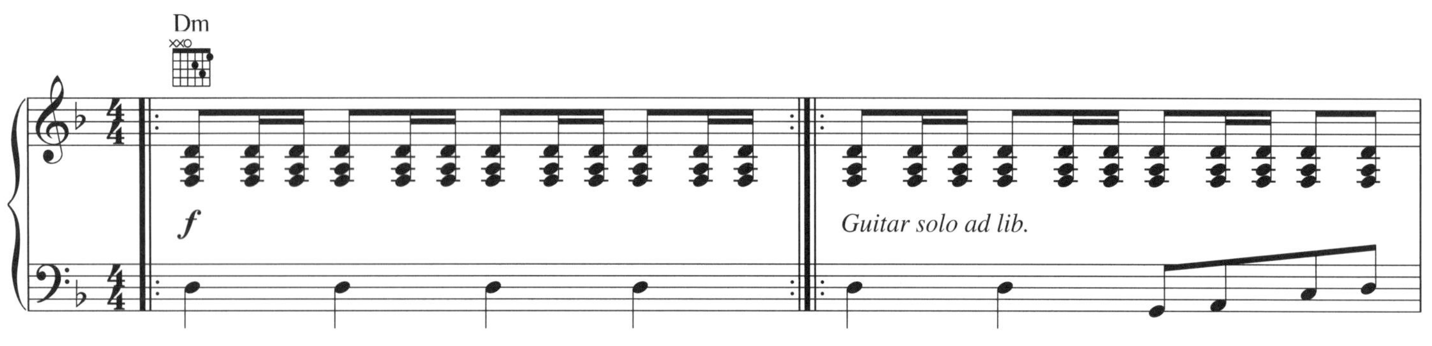
Dm
f
Guitar solo ad lib.

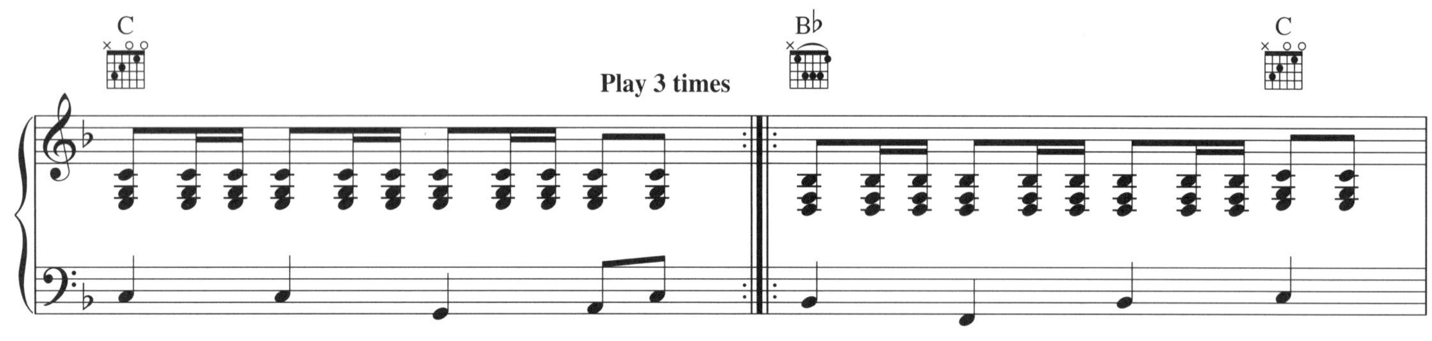
C
Play 3 times
B♭
C

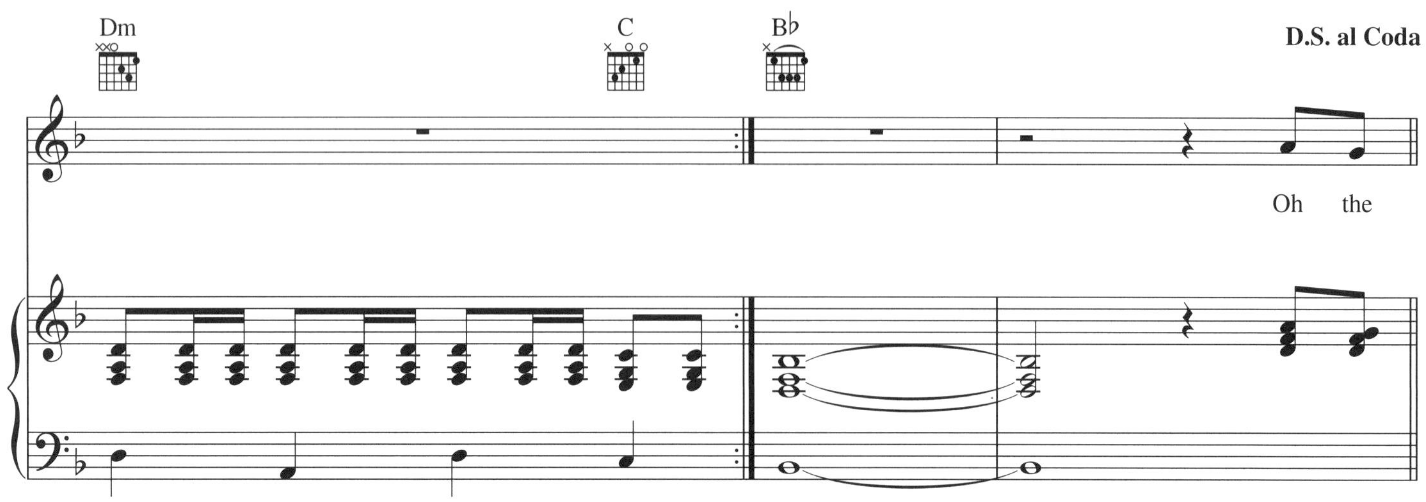
Dm
C
B♭
D.S. al Coda
Oh the

CODA
Dm
Oh, the
Dm
F
C
wheel in the sky keeps on turn - in' I
wheel in the sky keeps on turn - in' I
Dm
F
C
Play 4 times
don't know where I'll be to - mor - row.
don't know, I don't know I don't know.
B♭
Repeat and Fade
Optional Ending
B♭5

When You Love a Woman

Words and Music by
Steve Perry and Jonathan Cain
Music by Neal Schon

*Recorded a half step lower.

D
D/F♯
With - in my - self I was wrong.
I hope and pray to - night
My search - ing ain't
some - where you're
Gadd2
Asus4
A
o - ver,
think - ing of me, girl.
o - ver.
Yes, I know, I,
I know that
D
D/C♯
you see your world in - side her eyes.
(when you love a wom - an),
Bm
Bm/A
you know she's stand - ing by your side.
(When you love a wom - an),
(A

To Coda
Gmaj7
There's a band of gold that shines,
joy that lasts for - ev - er.)
Asus4
1.
A
wait - ing some - where.
Oh, yeah.
2.
A
G
Oh, it's e - nough to make you cry
Asus4
A
G
when you see her walk - ing by,

A
G
and you look in - to her eyes.
Asus4
A
Gadd2
Asus4
A
Woh, oh.
D
D/F♯
Bm7
A
D
D/F♯

D.S. al Coda
Bm
Asus4
A
Oh, oh, oh,
Coda
Asus4
D
woh, oh.
when you
(When you love a wom - an),
D/F♯
Bm
Freely
A
love, love, love, love,
(when you love a wom - an),
you see your
rit.
D
Bm7
D/F♯
Gadd2
D
world in - side her eyes.

Who's Crying Now

Words and Music by
Steve Perry and Jonathan Cain

G/F
Fmaj7
C/F
Dm7
and still they try to see
So man - y wrong or rights.
Em/D
E5
G5/E
Am
why some - thing good can hurt so bad.
Nei - ther could change their head - strong ways.
G/A
Am
G/A
Am
Caught on a
And in a
G/A
Fmaj7
G/F
Fmaj7
C/F
Dm7
3
one - way street,
lov - er's rage,
the taste of bit - ter - sweet;
they tore an - oth - er page.

Em/D
E5
G5/E
Am
love will sur - vive some - how, some
The fight - in' is worth the love they
way.
save.
G/A
Am
G/A
Am7
G/A
Fmaj7
G/F
Fmaj7
One love feeds the fire. One heart burns
C/F
Dm7
Em/D
Em/G
G
Am
de - sire. I won - der who's cry - ing now.

G/A
Am
G/A
Am7
3fr
Two hearts born
G/A
Fmaj7
G/F
Fmaj7
C/F
Dm7
to run.
Who'll be the lone - ly one?
Em/D
Em/G
G
Am7
1.
Am9
I won - der who's cry - ing now.
2.
Am9
On - ly
3

Fmaj7
Dm
Am
so many tears you can cry
Fmaj7
Dm7
till the heart-ache is o-ver. And
C
G
B♭
now you can say your love
Am
G/A
Am
G/A
Fmaj7
3fr
will nev-er die.

G/F
Fmaj7
C/F
Dm7
Em/D
E5
Woh, oh, oh, ooh,
G5/E
A5/E
Am
2fr
G/A
3fr
Am
oh, oh.
G/A
Am7
G/A
Fmaj7
G/F
Fmaj7
One love feeds the fire. One heart burns
C/F
Dm7
Em/D
E5
G5/E
A5/E
Am
de - sire. Won - der who's cry - ing now.

G/A
Am
G/A
Am7
Two hearts born
to run.
Fmaj7
G/F
Who'll be the lone-
C/F
Dm7
Em/D
Em/G
ly one?
I won - der who's
G
cry - ing now.
D.S. (instrumental) and fade

You Better Wait

Words and Music by
Steve Perry, George Hawkins,
Paul Taylor, Lincoln Brewster,
Moyes Lucas and John Pierce

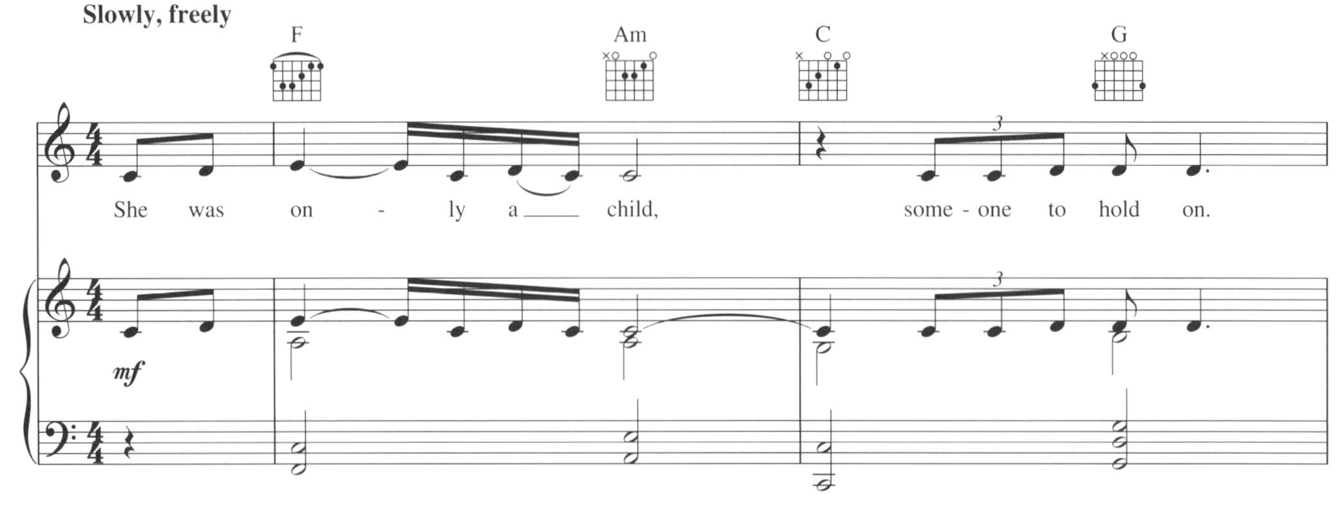

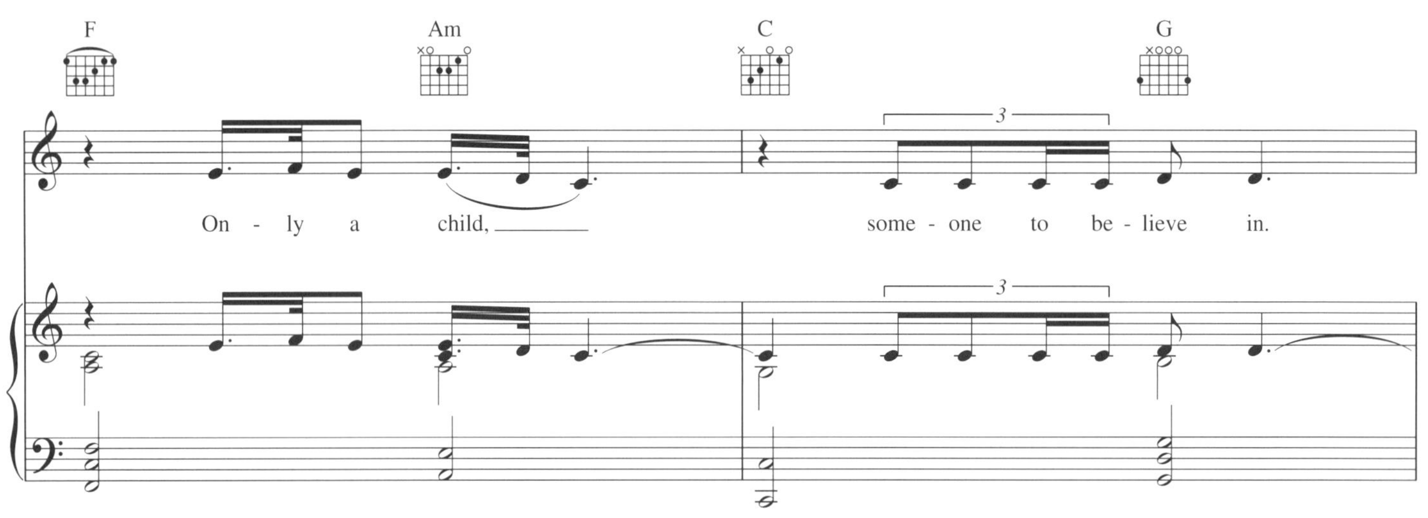

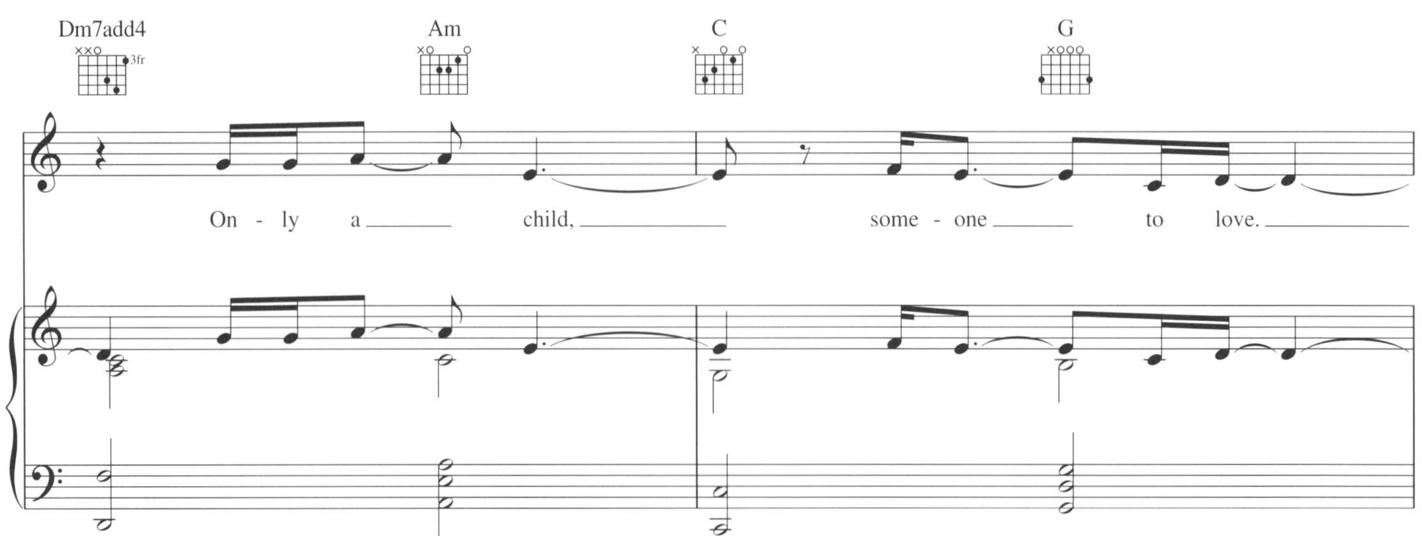

Em7add4
D
Am
Gsus4
G
D
Ah.
Moderately fast Rock
D
Am
C
1.
G
2.
G
D
Am
She was sev - en - teen,
beau - ty queen.
C
G
D
I met her in a mag - a - zine.
Heart of fi - re.

Am
C
G
Love's de - si - re, reach - in' out high - er, high - er.
D
Am
C
G
𝄋
D
Am
Run a - way one more day;
Pre - cious girl, lit - tle pearl,
C
G
a bro - ken - heart - ed child at play.
temp - ta - tion is a lone - ly world.

D
Am
I pray for you, ba - by blue.
Eyes de - ceive; they be - lieve
C
G
In the name of love, I reach for you.
in ev - 'ry - thing they wan - na see, yeah.
N.C.
In the dark - ness comes the e - vil of the night.
And the ne - on lights re - flect your light.
Think a - bout it.
On - ly you know where to hide, ba - by.
(You bet - ter

D
Dsus4
D
Am
wait.) Stop your - self be - fore you fall. (You bet - ter
C
G
D
wait.) Stop be - fore you lose it all. Some - where there's
Am
C
To Coda
G
love.
D
C/E
G
Csus2
Oh, some - where, some

C/E
D
D.S. al Coda
way.
Coda
G
D
(You bet - ter wait.) Stop yourself be -
Am
C
G
fore you start. (You bet - ter wait.) Don't look back. Don't lose heart.
N.C.

6
3
F
G/F
Don't look, don't look,
F
don't look back, babe.

D
Am
Csus2
G
D
Am
Csus2
G
G/F
3
Don't look,
don't look,
Freely
F
don't look back,
ba - by.

great songs series

Cherry Lane Music is proud to present this legendary series which has delighted players and performers for generations.

Great Songs of the Fifties

The latest release in Cherry Lane's acclaimed Great Songs series, this songbook presents 51 musical memories from the fabulous '50s! Features rock, pop, country, Broadway and movie tunes, including: All Shook Up • At the Hop • Blue Suede Shoes • Dream Lover • Fly Me to the Moon • Kansas City • Love Me Tender • Misty • Peggy Sue • Rock Around the Clock • Sea of Love • Sixteen Tons • Take the "A" Train • Wonderful! Wonderful! • and more. Includes an introduction by award-winning journalist Bruce Pollock.

_____02500323 P/V/G $16.95

Great Songs of the Sixties, Vol. 1 – Revised Edition

The newly updated version of this classic book includes 80 faves from the 1960s: Angel of the Morning • Bridge over Troubled Water • Cabaret • Different Drum • Do You Believe in Magic • Eve of Destruction • Georgy Girl • It Was a Very Good Year • Monday, Monday • People • Spinning Wheel • Walk on By • and more.

_____02509902 P/V/G $19.95

Great Songs of the Sixties, Vol. 2 – Revised Edition

61 more 60s hits: And When I Die • California Dreamin' • Crying • The 59th Street Bridge Song (Feelin' Groovy) • For Once in My Life • Honey • Little Green Apples • MacArthur Park • Me and Bobby McGee • Nowhere Man • Piece of My Heart • Sugar, Sugar • You Made Me So Very Happy • and more.

_____02509904 P/V/G $19.95

Great Songs of the Seventies – Revised Edition

This super collection of 70 big hits from the '70s includes: After the Love Has Gone • Afternoon Delight • Annie's Song • Band on the Run • Cold as Ice • FM • Imagine • It's Too Late • Layla • Let It Be • Maggie May • Piano Man • Shelter from the Storm • Superstar • Sweet Baby James • Time in a Bottle • The Way We Were • more!

_____02509917 P/V/G $19.95

Prices, contents, and availability subject to change without notice.

6 East 32nd Street, New York, NY 10016

Quality in Printed Music

Visit Cherry Lane on the Internet at
www.cherrylane.com

Great Songs of the Seventies – Volume 2

Features 58 outstanding '70s songs in rock, pop, country, Broadway and movie genres: American Woman • Baby, I'm-A Want You • Day by Day • Do That to Me One More Time • Dog & Butterfly • Don't Cry Out Loud • Dreamboat Annie • Follow Me • Get Closer • Grease • Heard It in a Love Song • I'll Be There • It's a Heartache • The Loco-Motion • My Eyes Adored You • New Kid in Town • Night Fever • On and On • Sing • Summer Breez[e] • Tonight's the Night • We Are the Champions • Y.M.C.A. • and more. Includes articles by Cherry Lane Music Company founder Milt Okun, and award-winning music journalist Bruce Pollock.

_____02500322 P/V/G $19.9

Great Songs of the Eighties – Revised Edition

This newly revised edition features 50 songs in roc[k] pop & country styles, plus hits from Broadway ar[nd] the movies! Songs: Almost Paradise • Angel of th[e] Morning • Do You Really Want to Hurt Me • Endle[ss] Love • Flashdance...What a Feeling • Guilty • Hung[ry] Eyes • (Just Like) Starting Over • Let Love Rule • Missing You • Patience • Through the Years • Tim[e] After Time • Total Eclipse of the Heart • and mor[e]

_____02502125 P/V/G $18.9

Great Songs of the Nineties

This terrific collection features 48 big hits in ma[ny] styles. Includes: Achy Breaky Heart • Beautiful [in] My Eyes • Believe • Black Hole Sun • Black Vel[vet] • Blaze of Glory • Building a Mystery • Crash i[nto] Me • Fields of Gold • From a Distance • Glyceri[ne] • Here and Now • Hold My Hand • I'll Make Lo[ve] to You • Ironic • Linger • My Heart Will Go On • Waterfalls • Wonderwall • and more.

_____02500040 P/V/G ....$16.

Great Songs of the Pop Era

Over 50 hits from the pop era, including: Amazed • Annie's Song • Ebony and Ivory • Every Breath Yo[u] Take • Hey Nineteen • I Want to Know What Love [Is] • I'm Every Woman • Just the Two of Us • Leavin[g] on a Jet Plane • My Cherie Amour • Raindrop[s] Keep Fallin' on My Head • Rocky Mountain High • This Is the Moment • Time After Time • (I've Had) the Time of My Life • What a Wonderful World • and more!

_____02500043 Easy Piano $16.9

Exclusively Distributed By

7777 W. Bluemound Rd. P.O. Box 13819 Milwaukee, WI 53213

040